Jacob Stole Esau's Blessing

Genesis: *Chapters 25:20—28:5*

After Abraham died, his son Isaac lived in the land of Canaan. Like his father, Isaac's home was a tent. Around him lived his people in tents and many flocks of sheep and herds of cattle.

Isaac and his wife Rebekah had twin sons. The older was named Esau and the younger Jacob. Esau was fond of hunting. He was rough and covered with hair. In contrast, Jacob was quiet and thoughtful. He liked staying at home and caring for the flocks of his father. Isaac loved Esau more than Jacob whereas Rebekah liked Jacob because he was wise and careful in his work.

In those lands at that time, when a man died his older son received twice as much as the younger of their father's property. This was called his 'birthright'. So Esau, would get more of Isaac's possessions than Jacob.

But when Esau grew up, he did not care for his birthright

or the blessing which God had promised. But Jacob who was wise, wished greatly to have the birthright which would come to Esau when his father died. One day, when Esau came home, hungry and tired from hunting, he saw Jacob having a bowl of something that he had just cooked for dinner. As Esau was hungry, he said, 'Will you not give me some, brother? I am hungry!'

'I will give it to you, if you will sell me your birthright,' said Jacob, cleverly.

Esau, who was not aware of his birthright, gave it away in return of some food!

The next moment, Esau made Jacob a solemn promise to give to Jacob his birthright that too for a bowl of food!

Many years passed and Isaac became very old and feeble. He became blind too. One day he said to Esau, 'My son, I am very old, and may die anytime. But before I die, I wish to give to you, as my older son, God's blessing upon you, and your children, and your descendants. Go out into the fields, hunt some animal and make me a dish out of it which I will love to eat. And after I have eaten it, I will give you the blessing.'

Esau, however, did not tell his father that he had sold his blessing to his brother Jacob.

Now Rebekah had heard their conversation, secretly. At once, she went and told Jacob what Isaac had told Esau. 'Now, my son,' said Rebekah, 'Do what I tell you. Bring me two little goat kids. I will cook them and then, you take it to your father. Thinking you to be Esau, he will give you his blessing.'

But Jacob said, 'Mother, you know that Esau and I are not completely alike. His neck and arms are covered with hair, while mine are smooth. Father will at once know that I am not Esau. And then, instead of giving me a blessing, he will curse me!'

But Rebekah said, 'Son, do as I have told you, and I will take care of you. Do not be afraid, but go and bring the meat.'

Jacob brought the kids and Rebekah made a dish from them in a manner that Isaac would like. Then Rebekah gave Jacob, Esau's clothes to wear. She also placed on his neck and hands some of the skin of the kids, to make his neck and hands hairy.

A little later, Jacob came into his father's tent with the dinner. 'Who are you, my son?' asked Isaac.

'I am Esau, your oldest son,' answered Jacob. 'I have done as you had told me. Now eat the dinner that I have made. And then, give me your blessings.'

As Isaac did not feel certain that it was his son Esau. So he said, 'Come nearer and let me feel you, so that I may know that you are really my son Esau.'

So Jacob went up to Isaac's bed, and Isaac felt his face, his neck, and his hands. He said, 'The voice sounds like Jacob, but the hands are like Esau's. Are you really my son Esau?' And Jacob lied again, 'I am father.'

Satisfied, old Isaac ate the food that Jacob had brought to him. Then, believing Jacob to be Esau, he gave him the blessing. As soon as Jacob had received the blessing, he left. He had scarcely left, when Esau came in with a dish prepared for his father. He said, 'Father, eat the food that I have brought and give me the blessing.' Isaac was surprised.

The poor, old man said, 'Who are you?' Esau answered confidently, 'I am your oldest son Esau.'

Old Isaac trembled and said, 'Who was that who came and brought food for me and to whom I have given my blessings?' When Esau heard this, he knew that he had been cheated and he cried aloud, 'O father, my brother has taken away my blessing, just as he took away my birthright! But can't you give me another blessing? Have you given everything to my brother?'

Isaac sadly told him all that he had said to Jacob. 'What is left for me to promise you, my son?'
But when Esau begged for another blessing Isaac blessed him with riches and power of the sword and many other good things!

Meanwhile, as Jacob knew that what he had done was wrong, he ran away to Haran, where his Uncle Laban lived. It was many years later that the two brothers reconciled and Esau forgave Jacob.

Years later, the people who came from Esau lived in a land called Edom on the south of the land of Israel, where Jacob's descendants also lived. It was better that Jacob's descendants had the blessing for Jacob's people worshipped God, and Esau's people worshipped idols and were wicked. But the truth remains that the way in which Jacob had obtained the blessing was extremely incorrect and immoral.